THE ROAD TO THE NFL

by Tim Green

SCHOLASTIC INC.

New York   Toronto   London   Auckland   Sydney
Mexico City   New Delhi   Hong Kong   Buenos Aires

Visit Scholastic.com for information about
our books and authors online!

ISBN 0-439-53816-5

Published by Scholastic Inc.
SCHOLASTIC and associated logos are trademarks and/or registered trademarks of Scholastic Inc.

12 11 10 9 8 7 6 5 4   3 4 5 6 7 8/0

Designed by Louise Bova
Printed in the U.S.A.
First Scholastic printing, August 2003

TABLE OF CONTENTS

Chapter One

MICHAEL VICK

Michael Vick is already one of the NFL's great quarterbacks. He can run and he can throw. In fact, some people think that he may be the fastest player in the league, while others think that no other quarterback can throw as hard or as well.

Michael grew up in Newport News, Virginia. He can remember going to his grandmother's house as a kid on the weekends and watching television. His grandmother had a floor-model TV. A floor-model TV is a big old piece of furniture. It looks like a chest of drawers, thick and tall, but instead of the top drawers, there's a TV.

Michael and his grandmother liked to watch the NFL. His grandmother was a Washington Redskins fan, so the whole family would watch the Redskins on Sunday afternoons.

When he was just seven years old, Michael stood up and told his grandmother, "I'm going to be an NFL player."

His grandmother just smiled.

When you are seven, no one thinks you are really going to be an NFL player. Being in the NFL is a dream, like going to the moon. It does not mean that you cannot do it; it just means that few people really get to do it. But Michael Vick held on tight to that dream.

The neighborhood where Michael and his family lived was a hard place to grow up. It was dangerous. Almost every night, from inside his bedroom, Michael could hear gunshots outside. There were criminals and gangs and drug dealers out on the streets. A lot of kids played and hung out on the streets, but not Michael. He had already decided that when he was in the NFL he would use the money he earned to move his mother and his grandmother out of this dangerous area.

Everyone in the neighborhood knew about Michael's dream and they wanted it to come true. So they watched to see that he did not get into trouble. His uncle Joseph kept a special eye on him. Joseph even made Michael play in his own yard, away from the trouble on the streets.

When Michael was eight, his mother sent him and his brother to the Boys & Girls Club. The Boys & Girls Club is where kids who live in cities can go to play sports and games after school or during summer vacation. Michael's mother wanted her boys to have fun and to stay out of trouble. She thought that sports at the Boys & Girls Club would help them do both, and she was right.

That year, the club was forming a flag football team. Flag football is just like NFL football except that the players do not tackle one another. Instead, players wear a belt with two thin flags hanging off it. When the player with the ball has a

flag pulled from his belt, it's just like being tackled in the NFL.

Michael joined the Boys Club Spartans, and their coach was Mr. Johnson. Coach Johnson asked the players which position they wanted to play. Michael wanted to be a wide receiver. He wanted to make diving catches. He wanted to score touchdowns. The problem was, *all* the boys wanted to play wide receiver. The team needed a quarterback.

"Who can play quarterback?" asked Coach Johnson.

Michael looked around. He wanted to be a receiver, but when his friend Wallace Green held up his hand to be the quarterback, Michael put his hand up, too. Wallace was a good athlete. He was older than Michael. But if Wallace could be a quarterback, then Michael thought he could be a quarterback, too.

Michael discovered that he loved playing quarterback. He was a good passer and he liked to call the plays. Michael's first game as quarterback was against a team called Oyster Point. On the first play of the game, Michael threw a touchdown pass. At that moment, Michael Vick knew for the first time that his dream really would come true: He would be an NFL player.

Warren Moon

He started to follow his favorite NFL players. He wanted to be like Warren Moon of the Houston Oilers, because Warren was one of the first black quarterbacks in the NFL. He wanted to be like Randall Cunningham of the Philadelphia Eagles, because Randall was the best running quarterback in the NFL. He also wanted to be like Steve Young of the San Francisco 49ers, because Steve was a famous left-handed quarterback, and Michael was left-handed, too.

Once, while he was still playing for the Spartans, Michael met NFL all-pro defensive end Bruce Smith. Bruce had come to talk to the boys about working hard in school and not using drugs. When Michael shook Bruce's hand, he dreamed that one day they would both be in the NFL and that they would be friends.

In high school, Michael had a coach who helped him become an even better quarterback. Coach Reamon made Michael lift lots of weights. Some quarterbacks do not like to lift weights. They think weights are just for the big linemen and linebackers, but Coach Reamon told Michael that a great quarterback needed to be strong. More important than that, a great quarterback needed to be fast.

When Michael finished high school, he accepted a scholarship to Virginia Tech. During his freshman year he learned that another thing a great quarterback needs is to be smart. During spring practice, he had a chance to compete for the starting quarterback position. Michael already knew that there were many plays in the playbook. But he decided that he had to know what every player did on every play. That way, he

Bruce Smith

would always know where his receivers were supposed to be when he was ready to throw the ball. So he studied the plays for hours and hours, and he watched a lot of film to see how the plays were run. He even began imagining that he was the quarterback in the film. Thanks to all this preparation, Michael learned to see things happen before they actually did—this is called read-ing a play, and it's a great skill for a quarter-back.

During those spring practices, the coaches were impressed with how well Michael knew the plays. They were also impressed with how well he threw and with his speed and his strength. But they also liked Michael, and that was important because a quarterback also has to be the leader of the team. They decided that Michael would be their first-string quarterback.

After just two years as the quarterback for Virginia Tech, Michael was the number-one pick in the NFL draft. The Atlanta Falcons picked him. Michael signed a contract and, just as he'd promised, he used that money to move his mother and his grandmother to a safe neigh-borhood. And, yes, Michael became good friends with his childhood idol, Bruce Smith.

Chapter Two

BRIAN URLACHER

People like to compare Brian Urlacher to a famous Chicago Bears linebacker named Dick Butkus. For many years, people said Dick Butkus was the best linebacker ever to play in the NFL. Brian Urlacher also plays for the Bears, and many people say Brian is the best linebacker in the NFL today.

Brian Urlacher was a young boy when his parents split up, and like all kids whose parents get divorced, Brian was very sad. At first he and his brother lived with their mom in Washington, D.C., but then the family moved to New Mexico. Suddenly, Brian had to make new friends and learn all about a new school and new teachers. It was a hard time.

A few years after they moved to New Mexico, Brian's mother married a man named Troy Leonard. Brian liked his new step-dad a lot. Brian and Troy enjoyed

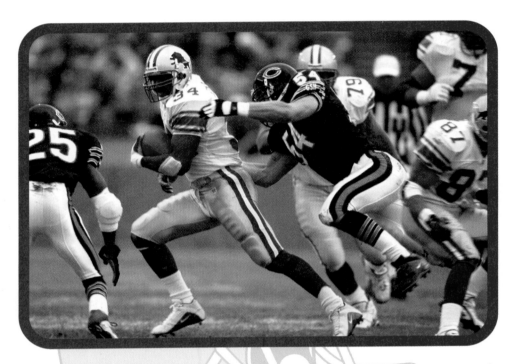

doing things together, and one of their favorite things was to watch NFL games on TV.

Troy's favorite team was the Dallas Cowboys, and the Cowboys became Brian's favorite team, too. His favorite players were Daryl "Moose" Johnston, the Cowboys' fullback, and Darren Woodson, the Cowboys' strong safety. Brian wanted to be like Moose and Darren, but there was one problem: Brian was too short and skinny. In fact, he was smaller than almost everyone in his grade. Brian thought that football players had to be big to play in the NFL.

However, even though he was small, Brian did play football. He'd play in the street with his brother and his friends. Usually, there were only three of them in the game. Brian would be the quarterback. He could throw and he could run. He was not big, but he was fast, *and* he was a good athlete.

When Brian was in sixth grade, he joined a flag football team. The next year he played on the middle school football team. That was the first time he played football in pads. Brian was an average player, and no one—not even Brian—thought he could ever play in the NFL. But Brian loved the game.

When he was fifteen, he was still too small to be a first-string player. Even so, he made 100 tackles in a season. The coaches knew he was a good tackler and they knew he was fast. They just wished he would grow.

When Brian was sixteen, he *did* grow. In two short years, he went from being the smallest boy in his grade to one of the

biggest. In his senior year in high school, he was six feet four inches tall. Because he wasn't big enough to play on a college football team until his senior year, the college scouts hadn't seen him play. In fact most college coaches did not even know Brian's name. Only one college, the University of New Mexico, offered Brian a football scholarship. However, when he got to college, Brian got even bigger. Soon he was

Dick Butkus

one of the best defensive players in the nation. He was faster than almost all the other players and played defensive back as well as linebacker.

In his last year of college, Brian was named to many All-America teams. Then the Chicago Bears drafted Brian. Even in his first season with the Bears, Brian was one of the best linebackers in the game. That was when people started calling him the new Dick Butkus, the greatest linebacker to ever play the game.

Chapter Three

DAVID DIXON

When David Dixon was a boy, he thought football was a game we in the United States call soccer. David grew up in New Zealand, an island country far away in the South Pacific Ocean. He lived in a small village an hour away from Auckland, New Zealand's capital city. While many people on the island trace their roots back to England, David is part of the Maori people who have lived on the island as far back as anyone can remember.

Most kids who grow up in New Zealand do not dream of being NFL football players, or even soccer players. They dream of becoming rugby players and being on a team called the All-Blacks. The All-Blacks wear black jerseys and they play against the best rugby teams from other countries. The New Zealand All-Blacks' biggest rivals are the Australians.

David was always big. When he was seventeen, he was six feet five inches tall and weighed 270 pounds. He was a star rugby player and helped the Junior All-Blacks beat the Australian Junior team in a big match. The entire country of New Zealand got excited about the victory.

Then one day, while David was walking down the main street in Auckland on his way to see a movie with his friends, a man stopped him. The man was a college football scout, and he was holding a tryout for New Zealand kids who wanted to go to America to play football. When he saw how big David was, he asked him to try out. He told David that if he was good enough, he could play football in college, then maybe go on to the NFL.

Three hundred kids showed up for the tryouts, but only two would get scholarships. David put on football pads for the first time. He ran sprints, hit sleds, and went through agility drills. David was fast for his size, and the scouts offered him a scholarship to Ricks Junior College in Idaho. David left New Zealand for America. He played so well on the defensive line at Ricks that he was offered a scholarship to Arizona State, a school with a big college football program. David was good enough to be drafted by the New England Patriots in the ninth round in 1992. But just weeks into summer training camp, he was cut.

David thought his dream of playing in the NFL was over. He went to work in Houston, Texas, as a boilermaker. It was hard work, putting together pipes that weighed thousands of pounds, but the work made David even bigger and even stronger. Then one day, he got a call from the Minnesota Vikings. David was so big, they thought he could play on the offensive line, even though he had played only defense in college. David agreed to try.

For three years he worked hard, learning his new position. Then, in his fourth year, 1997, David became a full-time starter for the Vikings. Even after nine years, he still plays there, living a dream he never even dreamed.

JEFF GARCIA

Like Joe Montana and Steve Young before him, Jeff Garcia is an all-pro quarterback for the San Francisco 49ers. Unlike Montana and Young, however, he did not play for a famous college team. In fact, he was not even drafted. For Jeff Garcia, everything seemed to happen the hard way.

Jeff's dad, Roberto, grew up on a farm. Roberto's parents

(Jeff's grandparents) were migrant farm workers from Mexico. When they finally got a small farm of their own, they wanted him to work on the farm, but he wanted to play football and go to college. However, Roberto did not have the money to pay for school, so Jeff's dad joined the Army. After serving his enlistment, Roberto had enough money for college. He went to

Gavilan Junior College and he played football there. After graduation, he went to Cal Poly San Luis Obispo and got a master's degree in teaching and coaching. Gavilan asked Roberto to come back and be the school's football coach.

Growing up, Jeff got to be around his father's team. He was the ball boy and started throwing passes on the sideline at an early age. At eight years old, he joined the Police Athletic League and played contact football, wearing pads, just like his father's players. He began to learn about the game from his dad. They would watch practice film together at home, shining the projector up on the wall.

The Oakland Raiders were the closest team to where the Garcias lived, and Jeff watched them on TV all the time. One day, some players from the Raiders and the San Francisco 49ers played a charity basketball game at the junior college. Jeff met Raiders greats Cliff Branch and Dave Casper. They gave him signed pho-

Cliff Branch

tographs of themselves playing football. Another time, Jeff and his family went on vacation and stayed in the same hotel as the Raiders. He saw Jim Plunkett and Ted Hendricks walking around in the halls. Jeff wanted to be like the NFL players he met, but he did not think he could. He was not a very big guy, and in his senior year of high school he broke his elbow and missed most of the season.

Eventually, Jeff went to play football for his dad at Gavilan. However, his dad already had a good quarterback, so Jeff spent his first year getting stronger. The next year, he played well. He still did not dream of the NFL. He wanted to be the best junior college player he could be. When he got a scholarship to San Jose State, he wanted to be the best small-school player he could be. His senior year in college, he was invited to an All-Star game called the East-West Shrine

Dave Casper

Game. Jeff played well and was named the game MVP. After that, he thought an NFL team would draft him, but no one did.

Instead, Jeff went to Calgary to play in the Canadian Football League. He was the backup quarterback behind Doug Flutie. The team was good, but Jeff sat on the bench. The next year, Flutie got hurt, and Jeff got to play. In his third year, Flutie left Calgary, allowing Garcia to be the starter. Two years after that, Jeff led Calgary to the CFL Championship. Finally, some NFL teams called him.

Jeff worked out for four different NFL teams, but he really wanted to play for the 49ers because they were so close to home. On his mother's birthday, Jeff got a call from Bill Walsh, the famous 49ers coach and general manager, offering him a contract. Jeff called his mom right away and said, "Happy birthday, Mom. I'm a Forty-niner."

Jeff's road was hard and long. But he had learned from his father's example that hard work could take him anywhere. Even to the NFL.

JOHN LYNCH

John Lynch and his father have the same name, and John wanted to be just like his dad, too. John's dad was drafted by the Pittsburgh Steelers. His dad was not with the Steelers for very long, but that did not matter to John.

With his football career over, John's dad moved to San Diego, California. When John was five, his dad and mom bought season tickets for the San Diego Chargers. John loved going to the games and cheering for the Chargers. Everyone who was a Chargers fan thought the Oakland Raiders were the bad guys. The Raiders wore black uniforms and they were a *really* good team. Even though the Chargers had a good team led by all-star quarterback Dan Fouts, they did not often beat the Raiders. But that did not matter to John. He loved football.

When he was eight, John began to play Pop Warner football. He was a linebacker on defense and a halfback on offense. When he was ten, John met his hero, Dan Fouts. Dan came to speak to the kids at the Boys & Girls Club sports awards night. Dan talked about how important sports were, but he also told the kids it was even more important to do well in school.

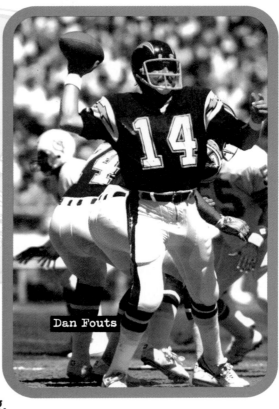

Dan Fouts

John had heard *those* words before. His dad always said the same thing, telling John and John's brother and sister that he wanted them to get only A's and B's in school. He knew John wanted to be an NFL player, and he told John that if he wanted to do that, he would have to go to college. To go to college, John's dad knew you had to have good grades in school.

When John got to high school, he played quarterback. He had a very strong arm and was a good passer. John's strong arm helped him to be good at something else, too. In addition to football, he was an all-star baseball pitcher. But John also worked hard at his classes, and he did well in school. In fact, he got a scholarship to Stanford University, the school many people call "The Harvard of the West."

At Stanford, the football coaches wanted John to play football, and the baseball coaches wanted him to play baseball. John decided to do both. In college football, players play either offense or defense. Because of his strong arm, John thought he should choose offense so he could play quarterback. For his first two years at college, John was the second-string quarterback. In baseball, however, he was a star player.

In his third year of college, John's football coaches told him he would have a better chance to play if he were a defensive player, so John stopped playing quarterback and began to play safety. Even in his third year, John did not make the first string, but in baseball, he continued to do well. After baseball season ended, the Florida Marlins drafted John. He signed a big contract and went to play for the Marlins. It looked like John's dream of playing in the NFL was not meant to be.

But in the fall, John went back to Stanford to finish school and to try to play football one last time. It was in his last year at college that John made the first string. Then things started to happen. Once he got to play, the coaches realized how good he was. Some people began to think that John was more than just a good baseball player. But was it too late? None of the pro scouts had even heard of John until his senior year. That meant he might not get drafted into the NFL.

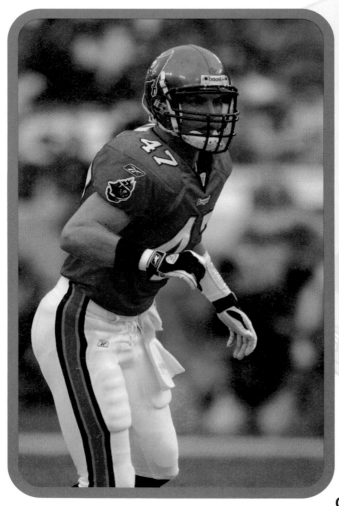

That spring, John went back to playing baseball with the Marlins. But all John could think about was whether the NFL would draft him. Then in April, John *was* drafted. The Tampa Bay Buccaneers picked him in the third round. Many of his friends said he should not bother with the NFL. He had a good career in front of him as a baseball player.

But John remembered that when he was a boy, he did not dream of playing baseball. He dreamed of playing football. He dreamed of being just like his dad.

Over the years, John became an NFL all-pro and one of the most famous defensive players in the league. Then, in January 2003, the Buccaneers went to the Super Bowl. The

Super Bowl that year was held in San Diego, John's hometown. The team they played were the bad guys from when John was a boy: the Oakland Raiders. Just like the Chargers when he was growing up, John's Buccaneers were the underdogs. Most people thought they would lose the Super Bowl. But that did not matter to John and his teammates. They believed that they could win, and they did. John was finally home.

Chapter Six

ANTHONY THOMAS

Unlike most NFL players, Anthony Thomas did not grow up playing football, or even watching it. He was a quiet kid who kept mostly to himself. His favorite place in the world was at home, in the kitchen. Anthony loved to be around his mom more than anyone. When his mom came home from work, Anthony would spend time with her in the kitchen, learning how to cook.

His mom taught him about different spices that made food taste good. She taught him how to measure things like flour and sugar without using a measuring cup. Anthony's mom measured cooking things with her bare hands and that's what she taught Anthony. And she told

him stories about how things were when she was a girl growing up. It was Anthony's favorite time.

Then, when Anthony was in the seventh grade, his mom told him that she had signed him up for the football team.

"I don't want to play football," Anthony said. "I want to be here with you."

Anthony's mom told him to try it.

"You need to get out of the house, Anthony," she said. "You need to find something to do. You need to be around the other boys."

Anthony still did not want to play, but he did what his mother told him. He became a wide receiver on the middle school team. Anthony played, but he was not very good. Still, he began to enjoy being on the football team and being around the other boys.

When Anthony was a high school freshman, the team's star running back was a senior whose first name was also Anthony. In the fifth game of the season Anthony Nash, the running back, hurt his ankle.

The coach asked Anthony Thomas to play running back instead. He had seen Anthony running in practice during the drills and thought he might do well. In his first game as a running back, Anthony ran for more than 150 yards. He scored two touchdowns.

After that, Anthony did not stop running until he had broken *all* the school records. In his senior year of high school, the

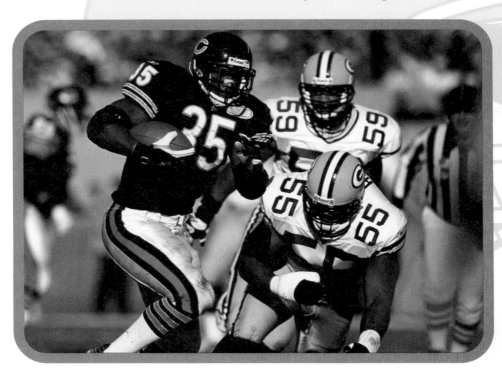

University of Michigan offered him a scholarship. Anthony was not very excited, but his mom told him he should play and go to college. Anthony went.

He became a star player at Michigan and was one of the best running backs in college football. At Michigan, Anthony would watch films of Barry Sanders. Barry played with the Detroit Lions, whose stadium was nearby. And he was one of the greatest NFL running backs ever. Anthony's coach told him he

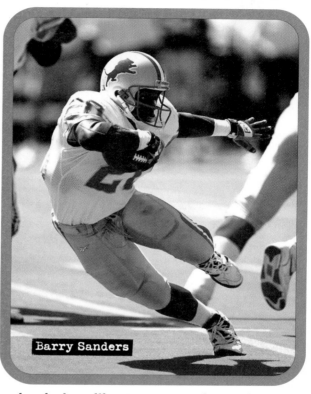

Barry Sanders

could be an NFL running back, just like Barry Sanders. That was the first time that Anthony thought about playing in the NFL. He worked even harder than he already did.

After his senior year, he was drafted in the second round by the Chicago Bears. When Anthony signed his contract, he took some of the money and bought a house. He and his wife, Hayley, live on the second floor. The first floor is for Anthony's mom. Even though he's a star running back in the NFL, Anthony still loves to be around his mom. And yes, she still does all the cooking.